WELCOME TO THE WORLD OF
Whales

Diane Swanson

WALRUS
BOOKS

Edited by Elizabeth McLean
Cover design by Steve Penner
Interior design by Margaret Ng
Typeset by Margaret Ng
Cover photograph by Victoria Hurst/First Light
Photo credits: Flip Nicklin/First Light vi, 4, 14, 22; Natural Selection/First Light 2, 24; D. Cheeseman/First Light 6; Bavaria/First Light 8; C. Allan Morgan/First Light 10, 26; Thomas Kitchin/First Light 12, 18, 20; Michael Baytoff/First Light 16

Printed and bound in Canada

Library and Archives Canada Cataloguing in Publication

Swanson, Diane, 1944–
　　Welcome to the world of whales

　　Includes index.
　　ISBN 1-55110-490-4
　　ISBN 978-1-55110-490-3

　　1. Whales—Juvenile literature. I. Title. II. Series.
QL737.C4S92 1996　　　j599.5　　C96-910369-7

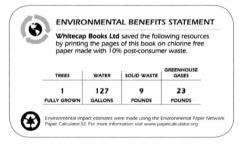

ENVIRONMENTAL BENEFITS STATEMENT

Whitecap Books Ltd saved the following resources by printing the pages of this book on chlorine free paper made with 10% post-consumer waste.

TREES	WATER	SOLID WASTE	GREENHOUSE GASES
1	127	9	23
FULLY GROWN	GALLONS	POUNDS	POUNDS

Environmental impact estimates were made using the Environmental Paper Network Paper Calculator 3.2. For more information visit www.papercalculator.org.

The publisher acknowledges the financial support of the Canada Council for the Arts, the British Columbia Arts Council, and the Government of Canada through the Canada Book Fund (CBF). Whitecap Books also acknowledges the financial support of the Province of British Columbia through the Book Publishing Tax Credit.

BRITISH COLUMBIA
ARTS COUNCIL

Canada Council　Conseil des Arts
for the Arts　　du Canada

Contents

World of Difference

WHALES ARE GIANTS,
WILD AND WET.

The biggest is the blue whale. It's longer than a basketball court, as heavy as 100 cars. Besides being the biggest whale, it's the biggest animal in the world.

Other giants include the fin whale— slimmer than the blue whale, but almost as long. The sperm whale is about the length of 3 cars. Its head, alone, is as long as 1 car. Even most dolphins and porpoises, which are types of small whales, grow at least as large as a man.

Swimming to the surface, the giant fin whale breathes through two blowholes set side by side.

1

Whales come in different colors, including gray, gray-blue, black, and white. Some are colored in patches. Others are spotted or speckled.

Although whales live in water, they're not fish. Whales are mammals—warm-blooded animals—like you. They can't breathe underwater.

The bottlenose dolphin is a toothed whale with a built-in smile.

No matter how deep they dive, they always return to the surface for air.

Whales jet stale air out of blowholes—nostrils in the tops of their heads. The spray of air looks like your breath on a cold day. Whales that have teeth have one blowhole each; toothless whales have two blowholes.

Before they dive under-water, all whales grab huge breaths of fresh air. Then they hold their breath by keeping their blowholes closed.

WONDER WHALES

Whales are amazing! Here are a few reasons why:
- Sperm whales can hold their breath for up to two hours.
- During its first year, the gray whale can gain half a kilogram (over a pound) an hour.
- The Atlantic white-sided dolphin has 120 to 132 teeth. Grown people have 32.
- The tongue of a blue whale can weigh as much as an elephant.

Where in the World

Traveling in a group, bottlenose dolphins search for food in shallow water.

THE WATER WORLD OF WHALES IS MOSTLY MADE OF SEAS. Whales travel all Earth's oceans. Some prefer deep water; others prefer shallow. Some whales also swim in rivers and lakes.

Different whales live off different coasts of North America. Narwhals and belugas live along the icy north coast of the Arctic. Some kinds of dolphins and porpoises live only off the Pacific coast; others, only off the Atlantic. The fin, sperm, blue, humpback, and killer whales (orcas) swim in both the Atlantic and Pacific Ocean—and in parts of the Arctic.

Tail up, the
humpback whale
dives down.
It's exploring its
summer home
in cold seas.

Once, gray whales lived off both the
Pacific and Atlantic coasts, but today,
they're just in the Pacific. Like many
whales, the gray whales travel north each
summer to feast in Arctic waters. In
winter, the grays head for warm Mexican
waters. There they mate and, about
12 months later, give birth. Their yearly

round trip is one of the longest made by any mammal in the world.

When whales get tired traveling, they take short naps. Some float with their backs just above water. Sleepily, they raise their heads to breathe, then drop them down.

At one time, many more whales—especially blue, sperm, and humpback whales—swam Earth's oceans. Today, only gray whales survive in their past numbers along the Pacific coast.

HOW WHALES CAME

Scientists believe that millions of years ago, whales lived on land. They were large, furry animals that walked on four legs.

Gradually, whales became sea creatures, built to live in water. They lost the fur coats that made swimming hard. They put on fat, called blubber, to keep them warm in cold seas. Their back legs disappeared; their front legs became flippers. And to make breathing easier, the whales' nostrils moved to the tops of their heads.

7

World of the Strainer

A cluster of snouts pokes through the water: the humpback whales are feeding.

MOST WHALES WITHOUT TEETH STRAIN FOOD FROM THE SEAS. Blue, fin, gray, and humpback whales use baleen—hundreds of long, thin plates that hang from their upper jaws. Baleen feels like fingernails, but one edge of each plate is bristly.

The whales suck in masses of water. With it come many small animals— especially shrimplike creatures called krill. When the whales force the water back out, the baleen traps the prey. Then the whales scrape it off with their tongues.

In Arctic summers, the krill group

The gray whale
has the shortest
baleen of all—only
30 centimetres
(1 foot) long.
Some whales
have baleen
12 times longer.

together so thickly they color the sea a reddish-brown. When the blue whale comes to feed, it gobbles up 40 million krill a day. Like the fin whale and other krill-feeders, the blue whale has pleats, or folds, of skin over its throat and chest. These pleats expand so the whale can suck in a lot of water and food at one time.

Sometimes, whales herd the krill close together before feeding. Then each big mouthful brims with food.

Most whales strain the surface of the sea, but gray whales feed along the bottom. They strain out water, sand, and mud, then swallow shrimp, clams, and fish. Gray whales also feed by forcing water from their mouths to stir up the sea bottom. Then they gulp down the animals that rise.

Top to bottom, the sea is worth straining.

FISHING WITH BUBBLES

Humpback whales sometimes use bubbles to catch fish. They puff air from their blowholes underwater. The air rises and forms a floating net of bubbles.

Flapping their flippers and blaring like trumpets, the humpback whales herd small fish toward the bubble net. Then up shoot the whales. With mouths wide open and throats fully stretched, they snatch the trapped fish. They strain out the water and gulp down their catch.

World of the Hunter

MOST WHALES WITH TEETH USE THEM FOR HUNTING. But their teeth are built for grabbing—not chewing. Sperm whales, belugas, porpoises, and dolphins (including killer whales) usually swallow food whole. Those that feed on larger prey, such as seals, swallow them in chunks.

Keen hearing helps whales hunt. But you won't spot their ears. They're tucked inside, and the openings to the inner ears are no bigger than a match tip. Still, a whale hears very well—much better than it sees or smells. Other parts of a whale's head also help it sense sound.

Killer whales are speedy hunters. They can travel as fast as race horses.

Kings once traded gold for cups made from narwhal teeth. They believed the teeth were magical.

The whale uses strong tail muscles to chase prey. By pumping its tail fins—called flukes—up and down, the whale swims well. It uses armlike flippers to steer itself.

Sometimes a killer whale senses seals lying on ice above water. It charges to the surface and bursts through the ice. Then it flings a seal into the sea and nabs it.

Some kinds of whales also hunt in teams. The killer whale's team is a pod—its family. Whacking the water with their heads and tails, the whales scare fish and herd them together. Then the pod forms a circle around the fish. One by one, each whale zooms into the circle and grabs some of the prey. In the world of the hunter, even young whales feed well.

LONG IN THE TOOTH

Imagine having a tooth more than half as long as your body. A male narwhal 5 metres (about 16 feet) long can grow a tooth 3 metres (about 10 feet) long. A female narwhal may grow a long tooth, too—but that's rare.

Coiled like a corkscrew, the tooth sticks out through the narwhal's top lip. It's usually the only tooth the whale has. A few narwhals have two teeth.

The long tooth may help a narwhal get a mate. It seems no use for hunting. Narwhals grab prey with their jaws.

World of Words

TRILLS, BARKS, SQUEALS, AND SQUEAKS. All whales make sounds. In their huge ocean homes, talking helps whales keep track of each other. It also helps them find their way and find their prey.

Toothed whales make sounds then listen for echoes—the sounds that bounce back off something. Echoes can help the whales learn the size and shape of another animal. They can also help the whales decide how far away that animal is and which way it's moving.

Each pod of killer whales speaks a

Every year, male humpback whales change the songs they sing—just a little.

17

language of its own. About 12 different calls help the whales get in touch and work together. When one pod talks to another pod, the whales often shriek like sirens.

Scientists don't think that baleen whales listen for echoes, but these whales

Belugas are the most talkative whales. Sometimes they sound like children shouting.

make many sounds. Some sigh softly; others sing loudly.

Male humpback whales sing louder than any other animal on Earth. Some of their songs last 30 minutes, and the whales sing them again and again. They might sing a love song to attract females. They might sing a scary song to frighten other males. Or they might sing a traveling song to contact each other. Along the coast, they swim far apart, so long-distance calls help humpbacks keep in touch.

A WHALE OF A CANARY

Belugas sing, whistle, and chirp, so early whale hunters named them "sea canaries." Sometimes, hundreds of belugas all sing together—like a giant canary choir.

But belugas make so many sounds that they could have many names. You might call them "sea dogs" because they bark and yip. Or you might call them "sea cows" because they also moo.

Some sounds have special meanings. Belugas seem to moan when they're afraid and trill when they're happy.

19

New World

TAIL FIRST IS HOW WHALES USUALLY ENTER THEIR WORLD. As soon as whale calves are born, their mothers urge them to the surface of the sea. Opening their blowholes, the calves grab their first breath of air.

Newborn whale calves are huge. A killer whale weighs about 180 kilograms (400 pounds) at birth; a blue whale, about a tonne (over a ton).

All calves are born hungry. They demand food right away. One may butt its mother and press against her belly to be fed. She squirts rich, creamy milk into

Killer whales are family animals. They feed, play, and travel as families year-round.

A humpback whale feeds her young calf about 40 times a day. A humpback may live 70 years.

its mouth again and again. It's a good thing she usually has only one calf at a time.

Whale calves grow fast. They put on thick layers of blubber, which help keep them warm. Depending on the kind of whale, they feed from their mothers for 6 to 24 months. All that time, the mothers—and some "babysitting" aunts—protect the calves from dangers, such as hungry sharks.

The calves keep busy. When they're not feeding, they practice swimming, holding their breath, and diving. They also spend time playing.

When a calf gets sleepy, it naps close beside its mother. It often rests its head against her. Sometimes a tired calf tries to climb on top of its mother. But whales are slippery, and the calf soon slides off.

Right after it takes its first breath, a newborn killer whale starts practicing swimming. Staying close to its mother, it moves back and forth underwater. It is able to hold its breath until it returns to the surface. But there it coughs and splutters. Breathing is something to practice, too.

Soon the newborn will talk. Like a human baby, it will learn by listening to its family. It will copy the whistles and clicks that fill its world.

Fun World

IT'S FUN TO PLAY IN WATER.
WHALES LIKE IT, TOO.

Dolphins like leaping over waves—
even waves made by ships as they nose
through the sea. But that can be a
dangerous game. If a dolphin isn't
careful, it might collide with the ship.

Some whales prefer quieter games.
They push and toss shells, seaweed—
almost anything that floats. One
big sperm whale was seen sailing a
wooden plank.

Whale calves play a lot. They swim,
dive, leap, and splash. Besides being fun,

Playful dolphins
burst from the
sea. Some flip
somersaults
before splashing
down.

25

A humpback whale leaps up to shake tiny animals off its body—and to have fun.

much of their play is great exercise. It helps the calves grow strong and healthy.

For safety, calves usually play near their mothers. Sometimes, they even play *with* their mothers. Gray whale families, for instance, have fun rubbing against each other.

Adult whales play with other adults, too. Killer whales like diving together. Sometimes they flip about suddenly and start chasing each other.

Grown belugas have a game they play over and over. One beluga dives to the sea floor and returns with a rock on its head. The others butt that beluga until the rock slides off. Then another beluga dives after a rock and starts the game all over again.

PEOPLE PLAYMATES

The sea is a whale playground. People who visit can get caught up in games. One humpback whale often swam close to the sides of ships. When passengers gathered to see it, the whale sprayed their faces.

Dolphins will often swim with a scuba diver underwater. Swooping up, down, or around, they do whatever the diver does. The more they play, the more they chatter—surrounding the diver with chirps and clicks.

Index